7777 W. BLUEMOUND RD. P.O. BOX 13819 MILWAUKEE, WI 53213

ISBN 978-1-61774-107-4

Published by:
Hal Leonard Corporation
7777 W. Bluemound Road
P.O. Box 13819
Milwaukee, WI 53213

Printed in the U.S.A.

Visit Hal Leonard Online at
www.halleonard.com

CONTENTS

INTRODUCTION

You like to sing, right?

You love the music of TV's hit show, GLEE, right?

How do we know? Well, because you've opened the book to this page.

The goal of the *Glee Vocal Method & Songbook* is to teach you how to become a better singer and performer in the style of GLEE, starting right now. So let's get singing.

Oops! One thing before you get started. If you want to make the most progress in the shortest amount of time, take a few minutes to read the next few paragraphs. The book and the companion CD work together and complement each other. (Think Rachel and Finn singing a duet in perfect harmony.)

The Book
- **Features eight of GLEE's most popular songs.**
- **Each song highlights three specific vocal concepts with three uniquely developed vocal exercises designed to build your "chops," the vocal skills needed to craft a great performance.**

Do the math: that's 24 key vocal skills. If you practice these skills, you can definitely become a better singer. But that's not all. You will also:
- **Learn the "language," the vocabulary of vocal study.**
- **Take "private lessons" with a professional vocal teacher.**
- **Sing in live performances with more experienced singers.**

What a terrific advantage for an aspiring singer!

Vocal skills are extremely important, but that's not the whole story... er, song. You must know what you are singing about. Discovering the emotional underpinning of the lyrics is crucial. More about that later. For now, let's discuss how to use the CD as part of your practice.

The CD
- **You join a vocal class with two other aspiring singers, taught by vocal coach (and co-author) Dr. Kate Reid.**
- **You practice each concept over and over with your "classmates" until you master all three concepts.**
- **There's a full-length version of all eight songs that you can practice and perform with.**

And guess what? This track sounds exactly like the original GLEE versions, except that there are no lead vocals. You get to do that.

- **As you are practicing, we'll assist you with guide melodies to help with rhythm and pitch.**
- **When you're ready to perform the GLEE song, the track has full cast of singers, supporting you just as you hear in every GLEE production.**

Let's go back to:

The Book

You'll find:

- **A brief background of the original artists and writers of each song**
- **The lyrics of the song (without music) for each chapter**
- **A short synopsis of what the song is about**

This is very important. You must be able to ask and answer the question, "What are we singing about?" In our professional work, we've found that the best singers are always good actors. As actors need to understand their characters, singers need to understand the emotional underpinnings of what they are singing.

Learning this process is one facet of crafting a great performance.

Another facet is choreography. You've watched every episode of GLEE, so you know everyone moves and dances to the music. If a guy in a wheelchair can move, so can you. We'll show you:

- **Choreography ideas for each song**
- **Guides for using microphones in your performance**
- **Staging ideas inspired by GLEE that are designed for as few as three singers up to 30 singers**

Exercise #1

TRACK 1

Possibly the single most important part of the *Glee Vocal Method & Songbook* is the GLEE vocal warm-up. Athletes warm up. Dancers warm up. Every great singer warms up. And you, too, need to warm up. Designed by Dr. Kate Reid, the GLEE vocal warm-up will help you prepare your voice for singing in this musical style. Track 1 of the CD has the GLEE vocal warm-up performed by the vocal class and Kate. Don't skip this. The warm-up is an essential building block to becoming a GLEE-worthy performer.

Start with this exercise to wake up the vocal instrument. Sing on the "mee" syllable and ascend in half-steps as shown below. As your voice begins to warm-up, change the syllable to one with a more open vowel, like "yoh."

The diaphragm is one of the muscles we use when we laugh. Try laughing a bit and see if you can feel it. Diaphragmatic breathing, in basic terms, involves the diaphragm muscle creating a vacuum from inhalation. While exhaling, the diaphragm slowly returns and helps us regulate the air we use to phonate when we speak or sing. With the proper diaphragmatic breath technique, you will likely feel the rib cage raising and the lower back muscles engaged.

On the breath pulse using the diaphragm, sing this exercise starting on a comfortable pitch, then ascend and descend.

Now let's use a "siren" to find a forward tone. The sound should resonate in the mask and mimic a siren. We are using the indefinite pitch symbol here because the goal of this exercise is to get an "up and over" feeling of resonating the sound forward in the mask, with the proper breath management and support.

In this next exercise, there should be no tension in your face, jaw, mouth, lips, shoulders, neck, etc. This exercise should be easy and relaxed.

Not all words in the English language begin with a consonant as shown in the previous exercises. Words or lyrics that begin with vowels present another important concept called "onset" or "attack." The way a tone is initiated on a vowel can affect its efficiency, quality, duration, and intonation. It is important to understand the difference between the three basic types of onset: balanced onset, glottal (hard attack), and the soft attack.

A **balanced onset** occurs when the vocal folds are brought together in conjunction with the application of the breath. This type of onset or attack does not engage the throat muscles but rather utilizes the diaphragmatic management of the air, along with the proper use of the vocal fold musculature.

A **glottal** (also called "glottal stop") or **hard attack** is heard when the vocalist initiates a tone by bringing the vocal folds together first and then applying the breath. The result is an explosive tone. This type of attack can be heard in regular speech as well. When overused in either speech or singing, it can cause vocal fatigue. Used sparingly and not exaggerated, this type of onset or attack can be effective in delivering a lyric. Be careful! An over-exaggerated glottal onset should never be required!

The **soft attack** is almost the direct opposite of the hard (glottal) attack. The soft attack occurs when too much air pressure is used and the vocal folds do not meet and close the space between them. The result of this type of attack is a breathy tone. This extreme, too, can cause vocal problems.

So now that you've practiced these exercises and are all warmed up, it's time to get started with Chapter 1.

Oh, wait... one more thing! Put a sticky note on these pages. You'll want to come back and warm up with these exercises every time before you sing.

Now, on your way—and have fun learning the *Glee Vocal Method*.

CHAPTER 1
Don't Stop Believin'

Song #1 "Don't Stop Believin'"

Words and Music by Steve Perry, Neal Schon and Jonathan Cain
Copyright ©1981 Lacey Boulevard Music (BMI) and Weed-High Nightmare Music (BMI)
All Rights for Weed-High Nightmare Music Administered by Wixen Music Publishing Inc.
International Copyright Secured   All Rights Reserved

The rock band Journey originally recorded this song in 1981. The song's writers were members of the band. Lead singer Steve Perry has said that the inspiration for "Don't Stop Believin'" came from the observations he made during Journey's Escape tour. Standing on his balcony in a downtown Detroit hotel at two o'clock in the morning, too hyped up after a show to sleep, Steve looked down and watched the activity below. The city was quiet, yet people were out in the streets with the echoes of conversations piercing the still, post-midnight air. Steve later told his bandmate Jonathan Cain that he saw those in the streets at that hour as "streetlight people." Jonathan Cain has said that his father gave him encouragement at a difficult time in his musical career when he told Jonathan not to get discouraged and "Don't stop believing."

Now, read the lyrics as sung by the cast of GLEE and develop your own connection to the emotional underpinnings of this story.

All: Dah, dah, dah, dah... (repeated until end of the song)

Boy: Just a small-town girl, livin' in a lonely world.
She took the midnight train goin' anywhere.

Girl: Just a city boy, born and raised in South Detroit.
He took the midnight train goin' anywhere.

Boy: A singer in a smoky room.

Girl: The smell of wine and cheap perfume.

Both: For a smile, they can share the night.
It goes on and on and on and on.

All: Strangers waiting up and down the boulevard,
Their shadows searching in the night.
Streetlight people, living just to find emotion,
Hiding somewhere in the night.

Girl: Workin' hard to get my fill.
Everybody wants a thrill.
Payin' anything to roll the dice
Just one more time.

Girl: Some will win, some will lose,
Some are born to sing the blues.
And oh, the movie never ends;
It goes on and on and on and on.

All: Strangers waiting up and down the boulevard,
Their shadows searching in the night.
Streetlight people, living just to find emotion,
Hiding somewhere in the night.

All: Don't stop believin';
Hold on to that feelin'.
Streetlight people.

All: Don't stop believin';
Hold on to that feelin'.
Streetlight people.

All: Don't stop!

GLEE Vocal Method #2
Key Concept: Group Diffused Tone

Okay! You've begun to develop your personal, emotional connection to the song, "Don't Stop Believin'." Now you're ready to jump into the vocal lesson, so let's get started with the group vocal intro.

This cool vocal sound almost feels like it's coming from an instrument. GLEE fans know that this opening reflects the musical transitions used in the show. Actually there's even a name for this somewhat instrumental quality. It's called "vocalise." It was popularized by a famous European vocal group known as the Swingle Singers. You might want to take a moment and Google the Swingle Singers, because their style is a key influence to the *Glee Vocal Method & Songbook*. Here's a hint: Vocalise style singing uses vowels rather than lyrics.

We call the cool, breathy tone production of the opening a *diffused* vocal sound.

At the beginning of this track, the ensemble produces a diffused tone for the background figures. This tone is generated by using a wide-shaped or lateral vowel "ah," with the sound resonating in the mouth. Hearing and feeling the difference between the forward "ee," the dropped-jaw tall "aw," and the lateral smile "ah" is vital to making this sound work in the group. Practice singing the forward focused "ee" to a taller "aw." Then sing from the "ee" to the lateral "ah." The difference in the sound and feel between the "ee" and the "ah" will be obvious if sung correctly. Proper mouth resonance, a flattened tongue, and a smile will result in the desired diffused tone.

Group Diffused Tone
Exercise #2

Next, sing the "ah" tone achieved from the exercise above with the syllable "dah." Make sure all voices in the group are matching the vowel shape and attacking each note with the same D.

Once you have worked on Exercise #2 in the book, fire up your boom box and join your CD "classmates" and vocal coach Dr. Kate Reid on CD Track 2.

You can practice and repeat this exercise over and over until you feel confident in your vocal delivery. When you're ready, this lesson segues into the vocal class singing only this section along with the fully produced track. Have fun singing along.

GLEE Vocal Method #3 —
Key Concept: Male Solo

We're going to work on the first male solo now. Finn's covered, somewhat breathy vocal quality is in contrast with the enunciation of the lyrics. He sounds like he's singing close to the microphone, which implies intimacy to the listener.

This tone and style is achieved by singing with a smaller space inside the mouth, by not exaggerating the diction or over-enunciating the vowels. When these lyrics are sung in the same manner that one would speak them, the cool gritty style is achieved. For example, you wouldn't say "Jahst a smawll town girl, living in aw lonely wo-orld" with all tall, dropped-jaw vowels. You would sing this as you say it. "Just a small town gurl, livin' in a lonely wur-urld."

It's also important to note that this gritty tone is often used when the male is required to sing in his upper register. Commonly used vowels in this style include "eh," "uh," "ay," and "ih." Practice singing these vowels sounds on the figures below.

Male Solo
Exercise #3

eh _____ uh _____ ay _____ ih _____

Women can also practice this exercise, though it will be more commonly found and heard in their speaking register.

eh _____ uh _____ ay _____ ih _____

Now that you have worked on Exercise #3 in the book, it's time to rejoin the vocal class as Kate coaches our aspiring male singer. Try to sing along with the lesson as Kate demonstrates the proper vocal production. This lesson segues into the solo section with the fully produced backing track for you to practice with. If you have any doubts about the rhythm and timing, listen for the guide melody that shows you exactly the correct rhythm and pitch.

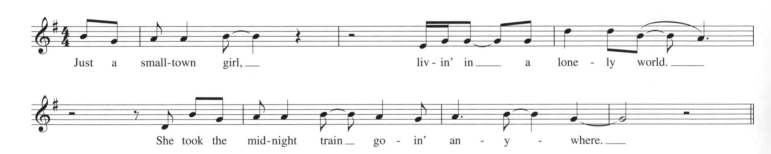

Just a small-town girl, ____ liv - in' in ____ a lone - ly world. ____

She took the mid-night train ____ go - in' an - y - where. ____

GLEE Vocal Method #4 ───────────
Key Concept: Female Forward Focus

Ladies, are you ready for your close-ups? No, make that your solos! The GLEE version features Rachel singing with her amazing bell-like clarity, which has its vocal heritage in Broadway stage singing. This exercise will help you develop your belt range—vocal that is, not waist size.

In order to achieve this aggressive vocal production based on speech, it is important to remember these four things:

- **Begin and project the tone using a diaphragmatic breath pulse.**
- **Maintain an open throat and relaxed jaw.**
- **Focus the sound in the mask.**
- **Approach peak notes in a musical phrase "up and over." Don't scoop.**

This exercise begins with the "me" syllable because the M already helps the nasal resonance. The "ee" vowel does the same thing, but adds duration to the tone. Practice these "siren sounds" and work for forward placement. The tone should resonate in the mask and mimic a siren sound. After you have mastered the "mee" syllable, change the vowel and continue to work on the forward placement of the resonance. This exercise can be used by male and female vocalists.

Female Forward Focus

mee _____ mee _____

The same technique applies to the next exercise. We continue the interval of a perfect fifth, but change the vowel on the middle tone, then return to "ee." Practice this exercise on different vowels, remembering to maintain the forward resonance and supporting the tone with proper breath management.

mee aw ee   mee aw ee

What are you waiting for? You've studied Exercise #4 in the book. The vocal class and Dr. Kate are ready for you to join them. Kate coaches the aspiring female singer on technique to get a vocal delivery that projects and yet maintains control. You know - how to get that bell-like vocal sound. Go ahead! Sing along with the lesson. You are, after all, an official member of the class!

This track also discusses techniques for singing the male-female duet, which immediately follows the female solo. The lesson segues into the solo section with the fully produced backing track for you to practice with. The track continues into the duet section. If you have any doubts about the rhythm and timing, listen for the guide melodies that show you and your duet singer exactly the correct rhythm and pitch.

GLEE Vocal Method #5 ———————————————
Full Performance – "Don't Stop Believin'"

As we promised at the start of this chapter, we want to immerse you in the GLEE vocal method. So let's jump right into a full performance of the song. (Or, as we like to call it, your "audition" to become an unofficial cast member on GLEE.)

The next item in the book is a professional lead sheet with the melody and ke y harmony notated exactly as it is for cast members on the show. So all you and the other singers need is a boom box or a computer and the *Glee Vocal Method*. That's it! That's all you need to put on your own performance. (Assuming, of course, that you've practiced and "rehearsed all the exercises.)

We have also included choreography ideas in the music to inspire you to create a complete performance. Okay, cue the band!

14

(Instrumental)

Just a
Just a

small town girl, ___ liv - in' in a lone - ly world. ___ She took the
cit - y boy, ___ born and raised in South De - troit. ___ He took the

mid - night train ___ go - in' an - y - where. ___
mid - night train ___ go - in' an - y - where. ___

(Instrumental)

A sing - er in a

smok - y room. ___ The smell of wine and cheap per - fume. ___ For a smile, ___ they can

share the night. It goes on and on ___ and on ___ and on. ___ Stran - gers ___
Street - light ___

wait - ing ___ up and down the boul - e - vard, ___ their shad - ows ___
peo - ple, ___ liv - ing just to find e - mo - tion, hid - ing ___

This track gives you the professional backing track to put on your own GLEE-worthy performance. Guide melodies are imbedded into the mix to help you find the correct rhythms and pitches. When the full casts sings, additional singers on the CD will support you. If your performance includes using a PA system, go to the last chapter of the book for a wealth of suggestions on working microphones into your performance.

But even with just a boom box, you're "Ready for Regionals."

Good luck and have fun.

CHAPTER 2
Keep Holding On

Song #2 "Keep Holding On"

Words and Music by Avril Lavigne and Lukasz Gottwald
Copyright © 2006 T C F Music Publishing, Inc., Almo Music Corp., Avril Lavigne Publishing Ltd. and Kasz Money Publishing
All Rights for Avril Lavigne Publishing Ltd. Controlled and Administered by Almo Music Corp.
All Rights for Kasz Money Publishing Controlled and Administered by Kobalt Music Publishing America, Inc.
All Rights Reserved Used by Permission

"Keep Holding On" was originally written as the closing theme for the 2006 fantasy adventure film *Eragon*. Avril Lavigne released it on her third album, ***The Damn Thing***, in 2007. The CD sold over a million copies worldwide and was certified as a Platinum CD.

GLEE's version of "Keep Holding On" features Rachel and Finn singing the main duet with the full support of the GLEE Vocal Ensemble. In this performance of the song, Rachel and Finn are offering emotional support to Quinn when she first discovers she is pregnant. Although the two are often rivals, when Rachel sings to Quinn, "You're not alone. Together we stand. I'll be by your side, you know I'll take your hand," we feel the camaraderie as Rachel's competitive personality turns compassionate and supportive. In Finn's solo he shows another way to be supportive as he sings, "When it gets cold and it feels like the end. There's no place to go, you know I won't give in." At the end of the song, the audience feels their emotional connection as the three GLEE Club members hold hands to show their solidarity and commitment to help Quinn through this difficult time.

For those who disparage popular music for its lack of depth, songs like "Keep Holding On" show the critics that certain contemporary writers of pop music can put great melodies and meaningful lyrics together. Avril Lavigne is one of today's music prodigies who speaks to her generation. In return, her generation has rewarded her with over 30 million record sales worldwide.

If you're a Gleek, you already know that the back-story of Quinn's pregnancy was a prominent element in the first season of GLEE. To craft a GLEE-worthy performance of this song, see if you can find the emotional feelings that come from showing your support to someone you know who is going through a challenging, life-changing situation.

> You're not alone.
> Together we stand.
> I'll be by your side, you know I'll take your hand.
> When it gets cold
> And it feels like the end,
> There's no place to go,
> You know I won't give in.
> No, I won't give in.
>
> Keep holding on,
> 'Cause you know we'll make it through, we'll make it through.
> Just stay strong,
> 'Cause you know I'm here for you, I'm here for you.
> There's nothing you can say,
> Nothing you can do.

There's no other way when it comes to the truth,
So keep holding on
'Cause you know we'll make it through, we'll make it through.

Keep holding on...
Keep holding on...

Now that you're feeling the compassion, the emotional strength, and the closeness this song conveys, let's work on the vocal techniques that can help you bring this song to life.

GLEE Vocal Method #6 ——————
Key Concept: Female Lower Register Singing
Keeping Your Performance Exciting in Your Low Range

Many pop songs start at a singer's lowest notes and build to higher, soaring melodies in the chorus. Performance-wise, that can be a vocal dilemma, because most singers find it hard to create an emotional performance in their lowest range. With a song like "Keep Holding On," the first few lines set the emotional stance for how the song will build. A great performance must capture the audience from the very first and very lowest notes of the song. The key to this kind of performance is maintaining an energized sound.

Female Lower Register
Exercise #6

Maintaining an energized sound is achieved by good breath support and maintaining the consistent air we have discussed previously. It is important to remember that singing in the lower register requires no pushing or forcing of the tone or voice. By relaxing, singing on lateral vowels, and maintaining a warm tone, you will achieve the intent of the lyric and style.

You're not a-lone.___ To-geth-er we stand.___ I'll be by your side, you know I'll take your_ hand.

Its time to cue your CD to Track 6 and join the class as they work with Kate on lower register singing for female singers.

GLEE Vocal Method #7 ——————
Key Concept: Breath Support for Singing Longer Phrases

When a melody has longer phrases, inexperienced singers often have problems trying to build breath support to sing through the entire melody line. Taking too many breaths at inappropriate times is one of the first clues that a performer is not ready for the GLEE Club or ready to be on the same stage with those singers from the Warblers.

Okay. Ready for some advice from one of the greatest pop singers of all time? You may have heard of Frank Sinatra. Before he became famous, he was the "boy singer" in a great 1940s big band called the Dorsey Brothers. Tommy Dorsey, the leader of the band, was a trombone player. When Frank Sinatra joined the band, he was blown away by the long phrases that Tommy Dorsey could play on the trombone. So, the instrumentalist taught the singer about breath support and how to apply brass player techniques to singing and phrasing. If Tommy Dorsey were here today, he would tell us what every brass player knows and what he taught Frank Sinatra: take in big amounts of air and then control the air as you sing each phrase.

Breath Support for Longer Phrases
Exercise #7

The topic of breath management and breathing technique is a vast one and there are many varying opinions on how to describe, teach, and build this integral aspect of singing. There is no question, however, that successful breath management and proper tone production is achieved by coordination of the inhalation, onset of the tone, duration of the phrase, and release of the tone.

The following basic vocal exercise from the GLEE warm-up page introduces several of these aspects and will help guide you through the fundamental concepts of proper breathing technique and breath management needed to sing and perform longer phrases.

Remember that diaphragmatic breathing, in basic terms, involves the diaphragm muscle creating a vacuum from the inhalation. The first measure of this exercise requires short and separated notes that allow for the practice of using this muscle. Each time you sing and release the pitch, you take another breath (that resets the diaphragm) and then as you exhale a little air, you again phonate and release. The second measure of the exercise requires the connection of the notes and addresses the duration of the phrase and release of a held note.

As you approach this exercise, work for a focused tone (thus the use of the "ee" vowel), not too much "h" in your onset, and good intonation.

Let's now join Kate and the class as they work on breath support and long phrase singing.

Cue your CD to Track 7 and take a big breath.

GLEE Vocal Method #8
Key Concept: Vocal Articulation

While we're still thinking like brass players, here's another key instrumental concept that we can apply to singing. It is called "articulation"—the attacks and releases with regard to the lyrics. Great singers know that singing to the end of the phrase is an essential element in crafting an outstanding performance. "Keep Holding On" presents the challenge of using breath releases for the long melodic lines that allow the words to come through and the tone to be strong and sung with conviction.

"Keep Holding On" is an excellent song for practicing tone and breath control as well as a meaningful reminder to keep holding onto the melody for the complete phrase. And here's the bonus: next time you see your friends who play brass instruments, you'll have a lot to talk about!

TRACK 8

Breath Control and Articulation
Exercise #8

Breath releases create both excitement and energy in a vocal line and are used in music genres including pop, jazz, and R&B. In this excerpt, merely place an aspirated H at the end of the held notes. Notice that the words "say" and "do" are held over the bar line to the first beat of the next measure. Be careful not to overdo this stylistic element, because it can distract from the integrity of the lyric and the melody.

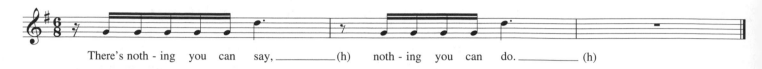

There's noth - ing you can say, _____ (h)   noth - ing you can do. _____ (h)

Let's join the class as they work on breath control and articulation. Cue your CD to Track 8.

TRACK 9

GLEE Vocal Method #9 ——————————
Full Performance – "Keep Holding On"

If you play a brass or a wind instrument, this song will be easier to perform. If you have diligently practiced the three main concepts for this song, you should be ready to turn your rehearsal into a great performance. Break a leg! Who knows? You may be the next Vocal Sensation!

CHAPTER 3
To Sir, With Love

Song #3 "To Sir, With Love"

Words by Don Black
Music by Marc London
© 1967 (Renewed 1995) SCREEN GEMS-EMI MUSIC INC.
All Rights Reserved International Copyright Secured Used by Permission

Paul Revere may have been an unwitting prophet when he trumpeted, "The British are coming! The British are coming!" In Chapter 4, we will talk about The Beatles and their influence on pop music. The international success of The Beatles on the music scene launched a wave of music artists from England that became known as "The British Invasion." The British Invasion included bands such The Rolling Stones, The Dave Clark Five, Herman's Hermits, and many others. Tom Jones, Petula Clark, and an artist named Lulu were among the many British solo singers who found fame on this side of The Pond.

In 1967, American movie star Sidney Poitier starred in a British film titled *To Sir, With Love*. Mr. Poitier played an idealistic teacher at an inner city London school. The movie wove together themes of social and racial issues, teenage cynicism and angst, and inspirational leadership. "To Sir, With Love" is the title song of the movie. Lulu, a young Scottish singer, sang the song and acted in the film. Lulu's recording became a #1 worldwide hit and transformed her into an international star. It's easy to see why GLEE used this song in its final episode of Season 1 when the entire New Directions vocal ensemble pays tribute to their teacher, Will Schuster, with a GLEE version of Lulu's hit.

As you read the lyrics excerpts from "To Sir, With Love," recall a favorite teacher or mentor who has been important in your life. Think about what they meant to you and try to make an emotional connection. Remember that at the heart of every great performance is the essential truth we call the "emotional underpinnings" of the story you are singing about.

> Those schoolgirl days of telling tales and biting nails are gone,
> But in my mind
> I know they will still live on and on.
> But how do you thank someone who has taken you from crayons to perfume
> Oh, it isn't easy, but I'll try.
>
> If you wanted the sky, I would write across the sky in letters
> That would soar a thousand feet high:
> "To sir, with love."

Do you understand "To Sir, With Love"? Do you have a personal connection you can relate to as you develop your performance?

GLEE Vocal Method #10
Key Concept: Relaxed Tone in Speaking Register

The GLEE version of "To Sir, With Love" is very faithful to Lulu's version. Lea Michele's character, Rachel Barry, fronts the ensemble with a quieter style of singing than her usual sing-to-the-last-row belting. Singing with a relaxed tone does not mean that your performance is boring. Great singers learn to bring the audience to them. Singing with a quieter tone is a great way to hook the audience into what you're singing about, especially with softer material. This next exercise will build control and intonation skills.

Singing with a Relaxed Tone
Exercise #10 A-B

Rachel sings this tune with a relaxed tone, partially due to the placement in her speaking register. This is generally an easier area of the voice to deliver a melody with proper breath support, resonance, and tone. The sound is not diffused or "airy," but the resonance is slightly lower than the nasal cavity or mask.

The first exercise is designed to show that the melody of the song can be relaxed and connected when sung on an "oo" vowel. Notice the slurs that indicate there are two phrases in this first set of lyrics, so only two breaths are needed. Sing this exercise with consistent air throughout the contour of the phrase.

A.

This time we add the lyrics. The trick here is that we still want to maintain the two phrases with forward energy, consistent air, and the contour of the phrase. Don't let the consonants in the lyric obstruct the phrase! Sing on the vowel and maintain the melodic line.

B.

Sssssh! Are you ready to sing softly with control and with great tone? Cue your CD to Track 10 and join Dr. Kate and the class.

GLEE Vocal Method #11
Key Concept: Wide Intervals and Intonation

We're going to tell you a studio secret. Even the best singers in the world struggle with intonation issues. It's one thing to sing in tune with an easy melody, especially a melody that hangs around a few notes. But in a song like "To Sir, With Love," the wider intervals make singing in tune a bigger challenge. In our experience, some singers have consistent intonation issues because of bad habits in how they approach intervals. They often rely on crutches such as scooping or excessive vibrato to jump from one note to another. Nothing will help you craft a GLEE-worthy performance more than singing in tune.

Wide Intervals and Intonation
Exercise #11 A-E

On an "ee" vowel, with a straight tone, sing each of these notes short and separated. While starting with a balanced onset, concentrate on singing in the middle of the pitch without scooping on the attack. Repeat this five-note exercise, starting a half step higher each time. Ascending chromatically allows you to explore the various areas of your vocal range. Be careful not to exceed your comfortable range. Always maintain proper breath support.

A.

The intervals get a little wider here, but the instruction is the same as above: repeat this exercise each time starting a half step higher. You can also descend starting a half step lower. Again, the various keys give you the opportunity to concentrate on vocal control and intonation in all parts of your range. Be careful not to exceed your comfortable range. Always maintain proper breath support.

B.

Same instruction as above, but remember to stay aware of the center of the pitch. Accuracy is vital!

C.

This time, connect the notes, still singing in the center of each pitch without scooping or affecting the attack.

D.

Again, sing these notes smooth and connected, always in the middle of the pitch. Avoid scoops and affectations of the attack.

E.

If you're ready to take your vocal chops to the next level, join Kate and the class as they work on intervallic singing and intonation. Cue your CD to Track 11 and listen to your voice improve.

GLEE Vocal Method #12 ————————————
Key Concept: The Intimate Vocal Sound

When we think about pop music or musical theater performances, we don't usually categorize these styles as being soft. But singing with an intimate approach has always been part of these styles. Even the biggest, loudest band or the most over-the-top Broadway show has a song that brings the audience closer by being performed quietly. Intimate performances need to be more than soft and sexy. Softer performances need to be effective in communicating the lyrics and the message, but in a different way than the loud rockers do it.

The Intimate Vocal Sound
Exercise #12

Creating an intimate feeling in a vocal line is achieved by a relaxed tone and by the treatment of the lyrics. You are telling a story when singing, and this performance by Rachel is no exception. The enunciation of the consonants, as well as the stress of the specific syllables, contributes to this type of emotional delivery. As you listen to Rachel's performance, notice where she stresses the lyric and how easily the words are heard and understood. She is singing this with extreme care, yet it feels like she's talking to a friend. As you practice this line, remember the tone exercise we worked on before and build upon that with the enunciation of the lyric and comfortable syllabic stress.

If you are ready to work on your intimate vocal performance skills, then cue your CD to Track 12 and work with Kate and the class—a little softer than usual this time.

GLEE Vocal Method #13 ————————————
Full Performance – "To Sir, With Love"

Some performers have built their entire careers on softer singing. Intimate ballads convey a completely different set of emotional clues to the audience. We like to make the distinction that softer performances are more like singing close to someone's ear versus louder performances that are more like singing to the entire theater. Bring the audience to you! You'll have them wanting more and more of your performance. Now cue up full performance Track 13 and pretend you're singing very closely to someone you love.

CHAPTER 4
Hello, Goodbye

Song #4 "Hello, Goodbye"

Baby Boomer Alert! Anyone falling into this category (and you know who you are) can skip this next paragraph. Telling you about The Beatles would be like preaching to the choir—or, in this case, the show choir. But for the rest of you youngsters, read on!

The Beatles were a musical tidal wave that swept across the Atlantic Ocean and changed music forever. Originally from Liverpool, England, the band became the best-selling recording artists in the world in the mid 1960s. Their phenomenal success became known as "Beatlemania." Almost 50 years later, The Beatles are still the most successful and the most artistic pop group of all time. Many of The Beatles' songs were contractually listed as being written "by John Lennon and Paul McCartney," but in reality these two rarely wrote together. "Hello, Goodbye," written by Paul McCartney, became a #1 hit from their 1967 *Magical Mystery Tour* album.

When Paul was interviewed about this song in 1967, he said that "Hello, Goodbye" was about duality: black and white, yes and no, hello and goodbye. McCartney explained, "The answer to everything is simple. It's a song about everything and nothing. If you have black, you have to have white. That's the amazing thing about life."

Now, read an excerpt from the lyrics as sung by the cast of GLEE. See if you can relate to Will Schuster's crumbling marriage as Finn and Rachel sing their solos that implies the duality in their complex relationship.

> You say yes, I say no.
> You say stop, and I say go, go, go.
> Oh, no.
> You say goodbye and I say hello,
> Hello, hello.
> I don't know why you say goodbye,
> I say hello.
> I say high, you say low.
> You say why, and I say I don't know.
> Oh, no.
> You say goodbye and I say hello,
> Hello, hello.

GLEE Vocal Method #14
Key Concept: Diphthongs

Diphthong—what a weird and strange sounding word—but one you need to add to your vocal vocabulary. (It's pronounced "DIFF-thong," but don't worry about the strange spelling. It won't be on the test.) Diphthongs are a common technique in pop music singing: linking two vowel sounds to pronounce a lyric. Diphthongs are also called "compound vowels." Lyrics such as house, oil, boy, and say all use diphthongs to fuse the vowel sounds to make pronunciation understandable. In "Hello, Goodbye," Rachel and Finn hold their vowel sounds for a long time and connect vowels as they sing "You say yes, I say no..."

One of the style elements of The Beatles is their fusion of American and British pronunciation idioms. The Beatles were influenced by American pop performers such as the Everly Brothers and Elvis Presley, yet their pronunciations often revealed their English accent. In the GLEE version, Finn and Rachel copy the vowel production of the Beatles as the sing, "You say yes, I say no... You say stop, and I say go, go, go. Oh, no." These lyrics need compound vowels to come alive.

Diphthongs
Exercise #14 A-B

Diphthongs: As you sing, hold onto the initial vowel sound of "no" and "go." Place the second vowel sound on the last beat just before you release the note and the word.

A.

Now put it into practice with lyric and melody from the song.

B.

You can practice this exercise until you feel confident in how diphthong production is formed with your mouth and tongue. When you're ready, join your classmates and Dr. Kate Reid on Track 14.

GLEE Vocal Method #15
Key Concept: Female Belting Tone

Now, take a deep breath and let's work on one of the most essential vocal production techniques for women singers, the female belting tone.

Here's some back-story—for those even older than Baby Boomers:

People have been singing songs forever. People using microphones and amplification to be heard, not quite as long. These "new-fangled" techniques arrived on the scene fairly recently—in "singer years," that is. Before amplification, singers needed to be heard by an audience of over a thousand people in a Broadway-style theater. They used their vocal production skills so that the audience could hear the lyrics clearly and be dramatically engaged in the performance.

The TV show GLEE is all about a type of performance that has its historical roots in musical theater and Broadway-style performing. This legacy is clearly apparent in the sound of Lea Michele, the actress who plays Rachel on GLEE. Her rise to stardom started on Broadway. She is a perfect example of a modern approach to a great tradition of superb lyric definition and projection of tone that we call "belting."

TRACK 15

Female Belting Tone
Exercise #15 A-B

In order to achieve this aggressive vocal production based on speech, it is important to remember these four things:

- **Begin and project the tone using a diaphragmatic breath pulse.**
- **Maintain an open throat and relaxed jaw.**
- **Focus the sound in the mask.**
- **Approach the peak notes in a musical phrase "up and over." Don't scoop.**

At first, speak this exercise without a given pitch. Start the breath pulse on beat 1 and say "hey" on beat 2, projecting the word as if you are trying to fill up the room. Start comfortably in your speaking register and place the speech tone forward in the mask of your face. Make sure the sound is not resonating in the throat and that you maintain a relaxed upper body, neck, and jaw. Repeat this exercise at higher pitches, remaining conscious of the proper technique outlined above. Remember, this is not a shout, but a controlled vocal production based on the breath pulse. Always stay in your comfortable range!

A.

Using the same technique from the exercise above, sing an ascending major third, this time connecting the pitches for a legato line. Still maintain the frontal placement of the tone, and use the breath pulse to start and keep the throat open and the jaw relaxed. This can also be repeated up in half steps in order to build your belt range. The same cautions apply in this exercise as in exercise A.

B.

Once you feel confident with this technique, cue your CD to Track 15 and join the class as Kate works with our soloist on female belting tone production. Remember that being an unofficial member of New Directions means that you can't be shy. Join Kate and our student singer and get ready to "belt it out!"

GLEE Vocal Method #16 ————
Key Concept: Unifying Vowels and Blending Timbres
with Proper Breath Support

Divas, take five. Some of the most exciting moments on GLEE are when the all the members of New Directions come together and sing as an ensemble. Singing in a group requires a completely different set of skills than being a diva or the star soloist.

The chorus to "Hello, Goodbye" is a great place to work on your ensemble chops. Ensemble singing requires vocal multi-tasking, singing and listening at the same time. And all the singers in the choir must agree to a unified approach in crafting the sound production, as well using proper breath support to keep the tone consistent and on pitch. Whew! That's a lot, but you can do it.

Unifying Vowels and Blending Timbres
Exercise #16 A-B

Group blending, unifying vowels
Work for these five concepts:

- **Unified vowel shape**
- **Agreement in the diphthongs**
- **Resonance**
- **Volume**
- **Level of diffused sound**

Begin with one singer performing this exercise. After he or she sings this once with the appropriate handling of our five vocal elements, keep repeating the exercise, each time adding another singer. As you continue to add more and more performers to the group sound, keep concentrating on the five vocal elements to maintain the proper blend and vocal sound. Sing this at a tempo that is comfortable for all performers involved.

A.

This exercise adds a rhythmic musical component and a faster vowel change.

B.

GLEE Vocal Method #17 ————
Full Performance – "Hello, Goodbye"

Okay! Soloists and divas, your break is over. The choir has practiced their unified approach to group singing. Now let's put it all together. Cue up Track 17 on you CD and lets perform the GLEE version of this classic by The Beatles, "Hello, Goodbye."

CHAPTER 5
Can't Fight This Feeling

Song #5 "Can't Fight This Feeling"

Words and Music by Kevin Cronin
Copyright ©1984 Fate Music (ASCAP)
International Copyright Secured All Rights Reserved

In Chapter 1, we discussed the great rock band, Journey. REO Speedwagon is also an '80s pop/ rock band that is still making music today. "Can't Fight This Feeling" is one of the songs they made famous. The lead singer of this band, Kevin Cronin, is also the songwriter for "Can't Fight This Feeling." The emotional setting for this song becomes apparent in the title. Kevin Cronin has said that his inspiration for writing the song was falling in love with a girl he had been friends with for a long time.

GLEE's version is very faithful to the overall sound of the original. Cory Monteith, who plays Finn Hudson on GLEE, delivers a great, slightly modernized version of REO Speedwagon's hit vocal with support from the GLEE choir on the choruses.

Read through the excerpts from the lyrics. Have you ever found yourself beginning to fall for someone who's been your friend, but now you see them in a different way? How did that make you feel?

> I can't fight this feeling any longer,
> And yet I'm still afraid to let it flow.
> What started out as friendship
> Has grown stronger,
> I only wish I had the strength to let it show.
>
> And even as I wander,
> I'm keeping you in sight.
> You're a candle in the window
> On a cold, dark winter's night.
>
> And I can't fight this feeling anymore.
> I've forgotten what I started fighting for.
> It's time to bring this ship into the shore
> And throw away the oars forever.
>
> 'Cause I can't fight this feeling anymore.
> I've forgotten what I started fighting for.
> Even if I have to crawl upon your floor,
> Come crashing through your door,
> Baby, I can't fight this feeling anymore.

Feeling awkward and confused? Great! Now you're ready to move on to the next exercise.

GLEE Vocal Method #18 ——————————
Key Concept: Straight Tone with Vocal Control

Singing with a straight tone is a little bit like walking on a high wire. It's easy to fall off the pitch. Many singers add a safety net of irrelevant and distracting vocal mannerisms—such as scoops and vibrato—to hide a singer's lack of control. Singing with a straight tone requires breath support and a consistent supply of air managed by the diaphragm to keep the tone sounding great and to achieve solid intonation. Work on this concept, because one of the best results can be a modern, hip sound that places the performance in a contemporary setting with many of the best of today's pop vocal artists.

Straight Tone with Vocal Control
Exercise #18

Vocal tone of any kind must be maintained with proper breath support and management. By this we mean that the inhalation uses the proper muscles, and those same muscles make certain the exhaled air is expelled at a steady rate. The diaphragm muscle that is used to inhale also assists in controlling exhalation. A straight tone, often used in pop and jazz vocal style, requires a steady stream of air as you exhale, as well as no change in vocal timbre, intonation, and vowel sound. This type of tone requires singing through to the end of either the word or phrase without wavering in pitch or pulsing the breath.

In this exercise, try holding a note for three beats without vibrato but with consistent air. Place your palm in front of your mouth as you sing and see if you can feel a little air (a little air is okay, too much and you're working with inefficient tone) being released at a consistent and steady rate. You can change the vowel, the consonant at the beginning of the syllable, and the note. Be aware that the change in register or part of the vocal range will affect the ease in which the exercise is achieved.

Okay, I think you're getting it. Cue up Track 18 and join the class as you, our student singer, and Kate work on straight-tone techniques.

GLEE Vocal Method #19 ——————————
Key Concept: Male Upper Range Placement

When it comes to male high notes, Chris Colfer's portrayal of Kurt Hummel gets the prize for hitting them dead on. But in this lesson, we're concentrating on male lead vocals more in the style of Finn. This is the sound that all pop singers need to develop, an expanded upper register that floats with consistency to the higher notes. With the right exercises, most men can sing higher than they believe possible. Opening up your high range requires moving the goal a little higher as you progress, much like working out in gym.

Male Upper Range Placement
Exercise #19

When working on the upper range, in any voice, it is important to note that all so-called "high" notes are part of the phrase as a whole. Be aware of the connection of all of the notes to the musical phrase, not just the higher pitches that make you anxious. Exercises that stretch or expand the vocal range should always begin in the comfortable zone of your voice and gradually extend by half steps into that part where it feels more difficult to produce a healthy tone quality with efficiency. Proper resonance that generally is placed forward in the mask and an awareness of the "weight" of the instrument are also vital to accessing the upper register in both men and women—and to expanding their voices.

We cannot stress enough that this is a process and, to some degree, is reliant on the sheer maturation (aging) of the voice. Take care not to "push" in these exercises and always note that discomfort when singing generally means that the vocal tone is not being produced properly.

Begin the following exercise on the syllable "nya," which sounds like the "gna" in the word "lasagna." As you ascend into the upper range, concentrate on the resonance placement and the "weightiness" of your singing. Don't sing too heavily in this exercise or you will not feel the benefit of it. Also note that your tone may lean toward what is considered a more "classical" sound. That is just fine! In fact, it is more preferred. The resonance will find its way more easily if you work for that forward, more "operatic" tone.

It's not just the men on GLEE who have set the bar for using their upper range in effortless and imaginative ways. Great rock singers such as Freddy Mercury of Queen and Steve Perry of Journey know how to do this. Pop/R&B singers such as Michael Jackson and brilliant crossover singers like Josh Groban also have mastered this technique. And you can, too. If you're ready to work out your upper range, join the class and get those high notes singin' by cueing up Track 18 on your CD.

GLEE Vocal Method #20
Key Concept: Speech-like Diction. Sing It Like You Say It.

Sometimes singers get so wrapped up in trying to get the melody out that they deliver convoluted phrasing of the words—making them sound like gibberish, even when we know what the words should be. As any fan of GLEE knows, the words are important in GLEE and the words are important in almost any type of vocal performance setting. Moving the dramatic storyline forward is often job one for a singer. In some modern music idioms such as rap, the vocal performer is given the storytelling job without the burden of carrying a melody. More traditional music styles can be made to sound more coherent by using a technique we call "sing it as you say it."

Sing It Like You Say It
TRACK 20 **Exercise #20**

The concept of "singing it as you say it" refers to the diction and modification or vowels to sound more like everyday speech. Words like "can't" are heard with a stopped T like "candt," "feeling" is sung "feelin," "forgotten" is now "forgottin," and "the" is really "thuh" rather than a long "thee." Use these diction tips to help you with this style element on the melody excerpt from "Can't Fight This Feeling."

I've for-got-tin what I start-id fight-in' for.

So what do you say (as you sing it)? The class is cued up Track 20 and waiting for you to join them.

GLEE Vocal Method #21
Full Performance – "Can't Fight This Feeling"

Now let's put all these concepts together: using straight tone with control and breath support, effortlessly placing those high notes, and bringing out the story with phrasing and coherent diction. Cue up Track 21. It's time for your close-up! Good luck! And have fun!

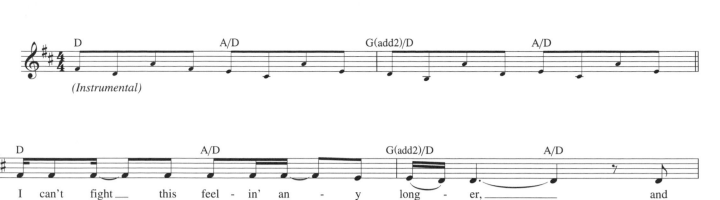

I can't fight ___ this feel - in' an - y long - er, _____ and

yet I'm still a - fraid ___ to let it flow. _____ What

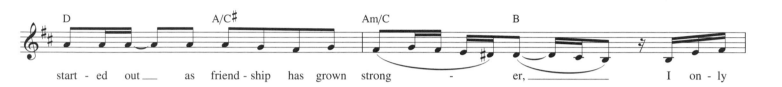

start - ed out ___ as friend - ship has grown strong - er, _____ I on - ly

wish I had ___ the strength to let it show. _____ And

e - ven as I wan - der, I'm keep - in' you ___ in sight. __ You're a

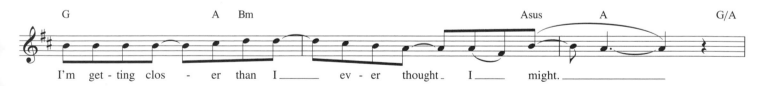

can - dle in the win - dow ___ on a cold, dark win - ter's night. _____ And

I'm get - ting clos - er than I _____ ev - er thought __ I _____ might. _____

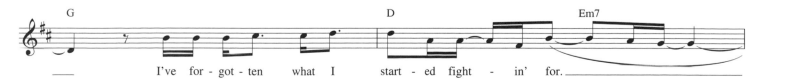

And I _____ can't fight ___ this feel - in' an - y - more. _____

___ I've for - got - ten what I start - ed fight - in' for. _____

CHAPTER 6
Lean on Me

Song #6 "Lean on Me"

This song has been one of the few in pop music to be a #1 hit with different versions recorded by different artists. When Bill Withers relocated from Slab Fork, West Virginia (population 202) to Los Angeles (population slightly more) to pursue his music career, he found that he missed the community ethic and the spirit of support that his small hometown gave him. This was the inspiration for "Lean on Me."

Because the song evokes a sense of supportive, empathetic feelings, various artists have performed "Lean on Me" for charity and fundraising events as well as on momentous occasions. Mary J. Blige performed "Lean on Me" at President Barack Obama's inaugural celebration in 2009.

The GLEE version is very faithful to the spirit of the Bill Withers original, except the chordal movement of the electric piano is now doubled by the gospel sounding group vocal. Making music often relies on "leaning on your choir mates." Now read these excerpts and find the emotional connection to this great pop/gospel song.

> Sometimes in our lives,
> We all have pain,
> We all have sorrow.
> But, if we are wise,
> We know that there's always tomorrow.
>
> Lean on me when you're not strong,
> And I'll be your friend,
> I'll help you carry on.
>
> You just call on me, brother, when you need a hand.
> We all need somebody to lean on.
> I just might have a problem that you'll understand.
> We all need somebody to lean on.

GLEE Vocal Method #22
Key Concept: Melismatic Singing

Are you feeling it? Feeling a connection to this song? Gospel-influenced music uses emotion to convey the song's message. There's a whole tool kit of techniques that great singers use to perform in this style. Here's one of them: It's called "melismatic singing" and it is uniquely indigenous to this style. This term refers to the gospel ornamentations great soulful singers such as Aretha Franklin, Etta James, Tina Turner, and Patti Labelle use to add to the basic melody and create their own version of a song. Of course on GLEE, the best soulful singer in New Directions is Mercedes, as played by singer/actress Amber Riley. Anyone aspiring to be a Gleek must learn to sing with melismatic, gospel ornamentation. So read on...

Oh, by the way, it's not just the Gleeks who rely on this technique as an essential embellishment to their vocal styling—think Mariah Carey and Christina Aguilera.

Anyway, in the GLEE version of "Lean on Me," the main opening duet is between Will Schuster and Rachel Barry, neither of whom is a singer in the black gospel tradition that Mercedes exemplifies. But all the GLEE singers use this influence in their own way. When Mercedes takes over on the second verse on the GLEE version, you can really hear a singer influenced by Aretha, Patti, Tina, and Mariah.

Melismatic Singing
Exercise #22 A-B

A melisma is the singing of a single syllable of text while moving between several notes in succession. It is a style trait characteristic of pop and gospel music. Singing melismas requires vocal agility with proper breath support. The following exercise assists this necessary vocal flexibility. Choose a tempo that allows consistency in the performance of the 16th notes on a syllable and pitch that is comfortable for you. Be careful not to oversing or sing heavily with too much air. As you get more comfortable with the tempo, continue to increase the metronome marking while raising the pitch. Remember to keep the 16th notes even as you sing. As you get more comfortable with this pattern, add some vibrato to the tone.

A.

These next two musical examples are melismatic ornaments that are sung in "Lean on Me." Choose a comfortable and natural syllable or "mm" and sing these ideas over until the motive is in your ear. The more relaxed you are with the notes, the more natural it will become. These are often improvised figures, so feel free to come up with your own. Listen to the track for more ideas. Remember to avoid tension in the sound. You need to keep the jaw relaxed.

B.

Once you feel confident with these techniques, fire up your CD playing machine and cue to Track 22 and join the class as Dr. Kate works with our soloists on melismatic and gospel ornamentations. Remember that you don't have to be black, brown, or green to sing soulfully. Learning these vocal embellishment techniques will put you on the road to becoming a better, more agile vocalist.

GLEE Vocal Method #23 ———
Key Concept: Gospel Vibrato

Vibrato is one of the most powerfully emotive tools a singer possesses to craft an amazing performance. But it also can be weapon of musical mass destruction. Learning to use and control vibrato is an essential step in becoming a GLEE-worthy singer.

We're going to focus this lesson on gospel vibrato, because most gospel and R&B-influenced performances on GLEE use individual variation on this technique.

The GLEE vocal style of the various cast members is not imbued with overly heavy or wide vibrato, but almost all the ensemble singing features a certain amount of vibrato. Finn, for instance, uses very little; Rachel uses a more Broadway version; so does Kurt. Britney, Mark, and Quinn have almost a straight tone. But Mercedes (aka Amber Riley) uses vibrato in the classic tradition of Aretha Franklin, Etta James, Patti Labelle, and other incredible singers. That's the sound we're going to focus on as we study "Lean on Me" with Kate.

Gospel Vibrato
Exercise #23 A-B

Gospel vibrato generally is produced on lateral vowels with a flatter tongue over long, held notes. The vibrato tends to be faster than other vocal styles like pop and jazz, but the rate of pulsation is slower than the vibrato when singing various types of choral or classical literature. Generally, the interval distance between the two tones in the vibrato pulsation is a half step. Begin this exercise on the word "yeah" and go right to the vowel sound in the word "cat." The tone is sustained with consistent air and should resonate a bit more forward in the mask and nasal cavity.

A.

In "Lean on Me," notice that Mercedes doesn't use constant vibrato on every held note or every note or word in a phrase. Rather, she uses vibrato as a decoration or embellishment. Although vibrato helps to define the gospel style, one must be careful not to overuse it! You can use your ears and decide where the vibrato is appropriate and effective. Here are some ideas! We'll use this symbol to indicate vibrato.

B.

Dr. Kate, the students are ready to perfect their vibrato technique in the style of GLEE. They've cued their CDs to Track 23 and are eager to join your class.

GLEE Vocal Method #24
Key Concept: Groove and feel. "Singing in the Pocket"

When we say "singing in the pocket," we don't mean vocalizing that's coming from your jacket. We're talking about the special synchronicity that happens when singers generate time/tempo feel together. Maybe some singers are born with the natural facility to create rhythmic pulse from their vocal performance, but we find that most singers need to work on the method of time creation. And work on it they should, because it is a huge part of singing pop music.

We usually attribute time and rhythmic pulse to rhythm section players such as drummers, bassists, guitarists, and keyboard players. But singing, at its fundamental essence, is about generating time and feel.

"Singing in the pocket" is something that classical music choirs may find somewhat foreign. It does not relate to reading the music exactly as written. It has more to do with establishing a common interpretation of the sub-pulse feel of the music by all the choir members. The sub-pulse is the feeling that supports the strong beats of 1 and 3 or 2 and 4 that often are the eighth notes and 16th notes underlying the feel of a song. One of the best ways to find the pocket is to listen to the hi-hat cymbal in a drum set or the guitar rhythms that play behind the vocal. When a group of singers can generate this feel, the resulting "singing in the pocket" can be one of the most powerful sensations in vocal music.

Singing in the Pocket
Exercise #24 A-B

The subdivision of the eighth note is vital to "singing in the pocket" on "Lean on Me." It is vital to remember that all the vocal articulation (attacks and releases) must occur with the subdivision in mind. The use of a metronome for these exercises is helpful, although not entirely necessary. In this first exercise, you can set the metronome for the eighth notes and clap on the quarter notes—beats 2 and 4. If you don't have a metronome, you can use the instrumental track on the CD or practice this along with the GLEE soundtrack. The emphasis here is on feeling the center of the beat to "sit" right in the middle of each beat. This is also a great group exercise, just getting everyone's ears together.

As you consider the subdivision and the strong pulses on beats 2 and 4, add the vocal line of the melody. Be aware of the placement of consonants in your attacks and releases, as well as the vibrato. Note where the vocal melody lines up with the subdivision of the eighth note. If possible, clap on beats 2 and 4 while you sing. A metronome is always helpful!

Lean on __ me __ when you're not strong, __ and I'll be your friend, __ I'll help you car-

Are you feeling the beat? Can you find the sub-pulse? Now cue your CD to Track 24 and join the class as they work with you to "sing in the pocket."

GLEE Vocal Method #25 ————————————————
Full Performance – "Lean on Me"

We think that the skills learned from "Lean on Me" are some of the most important in the entire GLEE Vocal Method. (But that doesn't mean you can skip the rest of the chapters.) Learning ornamentation, gospel-influenced vibrato, and singing in the pocket are huge concepts that will help any singer at any skill level. The GLEE cast has performed music in almost every possible genre, but singing under the influence of gospel music is at the heart and soul of almost all American music styles. So, cue up your CD and sing with our full ensemble on "Lean on Me."

CHAPTER 7
Sing!

Song #7 "Sing!"

Now that you're 25 vocal exercises into the *Glee Vocal Method & Songbook*, isn't it ironic that this song and the accompanying lessons feature a performance that is all about *not* singing?

In the GLEE version of "Sing," from the Broadway musical *A Chorus Line*, Tina (Jenna Ushkowitz) challenges Mike (Harry Shum Jr.) to sing.

As GLEE fans know, Mike is an amazing dancer who doesn't really sing on GLEE. Kudos to producer/director Ryan Murphy and his GLEE team for using this song as a dramatic device. Not only does it move the GLEE storyline forward, but it's also an innovative way to connect a new generation of viewers to one of America's most treasured art forms, the Broadway musical.

In 1975, *A Chorus Line* opened on Broadway. It won a Pulitzer Prize for drama and nine Tony awards. The show has 19 main characters and is set on the bare stage of a Broadway theater during an audition for a new musical. The actual lives of Broadway singer/dancers—or, as they are sometimes called, "gypsies," make up the storyline and motivate the narrative of this classic musical. In the original production, Kristine, a rather tone-deaf, scatterbrained dancer, performs the non-singing role. As Kristine laments that she could never sing, her husband interrupts her, finishing her phrases with perfectly in-tune singing. GLEE reverses the roles, with Mike as the non-singer and Tina as the in-tune Broadway diva.

Bet you might be wondering why a chapter on "not singing" should be included in a book about singing. Here's the answer: Ever present in the dramatic storyline of GLEE is the desire of everyone in New Directions to put on a great show. While not every singer has the amazing vocal agility of Rachel Berry, they all strive to make a contribution by giving the best they have to offer. So, this chapter is all about looking to the great tradition of musical theater to craft a performance and entertain the audience.

And here's something interesting: Not all great Broadway musical performers are great singers. In fact many classic Broadway performers were marginal singers but wonderful performers. Do you remember the musical, *My Fair Lady*? The lead role of Professor Henry Higgins was played by Rex Harrison, a terrific actor but a so-so singer. To make the best of his limited vocal ability, the creators of this musical developed a style of "speak singing" that is a major part of many legendary Broadway performances. Another example is Robert Preston's show-stopping performance of "Ya Got Trouble" in *The Music Man*. Robert Preston almost didn't get the part of Harold Hill because the producers were concerned about his lack of singing ability. A non-singing actor playing the role of a music man—how could that possibly work? But Robert Preston's incredible talk-singing audition of "Ya Got Trouble" showed them how, and won him the role and the hearts of theatergoers.

Tina and Mike's performance of "Sing!" is in that same tradition. Mike can't really sing and Tina finishes his every thought with perfect intonation. Together they evoke a performance that is more than a song—it's entertainment! For anyone wanting to be a Broadway performer, becoming an entertainer is the most important concept.

Study the lyrics excerpts from "Sing!" As you read them, try to imagine which character you would play. Think of how you could perform this fantastic song.

MIKE	TINA
Hey, when I begin to...	shreik,
It's a cross between a...	squeak,
And a quiver or a...	moan.
It's a little like a...	croak,
Or the record player...	broke.
What it doesn't have is...	tone.
Oh, I know you're thinking,	
What a crazy...	ding-a-ling!
But I really couldn't...	sing.
I could never really...	sing.
What I couldn't do was...	sing!

GLEE Vocal Method #26 —
Key Concept: Musical Theater Character Voice Speak-Singing

Speak-singing is a great Broadway performance tradition. In this chapter we're going to break down some of the techniques needed to speak-sing. Projection is an important component of speak-singing, because conversational talking won't project in a way that the audience will hear and understand. Almost every Broadway speak-singing song is set to rhythm similar to singing—it's just not performed to a specific musical pitch. This first exercise suggests ways to practice excited energized speaking in rhythm.

Speak-Singing
Exercise #26

"Speak-singing" is a term we use that refers to a vocal performance on unassigned pitches that has speech-like inflections, logical syllabic stress and that does not sound trained. As this type of vocal performance is used in musical theater literature, it is vital to the development of a character and the delivery of his or her "voice." Consider the context in which the text is being delivered. If the character is conveying a lot of excitement or energy, you probably will need to raise the speaking pitch of the line. Take this first line of "Sing!" and practice the lyric, moving the text line up and down in pitch, as you would actually say these words. Try accenting different words and hear how the meaning of the text might change.

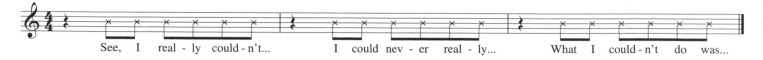

Are you speak-singing with enunciation? Can they hear you in the last row of the theater? How about the balcony? All right, then you're ready cue your CD to ID #26 and join Kate and the thespians as they develop this important facet of stage performance.

GLEE Vocal Method #27 ——————————————
Key Concept: Enunciation

Have you ever tried to have a conversation with a person, but you couldn't understand what they were saying? How long did you stay interested? As a performer in the style of GLEE, every moment you're onstage requires attention to enunciation—clearly pronouncing syllables, especially consonants, so that the audience understands you. The very foundation of any performance demands that the audience hears what you are saying and understands the words you're singing. Certain rock'n'roll and folk performers have a dubious reputation for their vague enunciation style. That won't cut it on Broadway or on a musical performance stage anywhere. This lesson is all about moving your mouth in a way to bring clarity to the words you're saying and singing.

TRACK 27

Enunciation
Exercise #27

Using the same phrase from "Sing!," concentrate on the consonants as you practice it. Give a little more time on the R in "really," the C in "couldn't," the N in "never," the W in "what" and "was," the D in "do." This type of enunciation, along with the character style inflections of the line, helps us achieve the clarity and intelligibility of the lyric and storyline.

See, I real-ly could-n't...   I could nev-er real-ly...   What I could-n't do was...

Got that mouth moving and syllables flying? It's time to join the class as Kate and the group work on enunciation. Cue up your CD to Track 27—no mumbling allowed.

GLEE Vocal Method #28 ——————————————
Key Concept: Projection

Putting your character's speak-singing together with great enunciation is an important step along the road to building a GLEE-worthy performance. Some performers do both of these concepts right, but fail to project. This lesson and exercise focuses on how to put many facets of your craft together to project. Breath control, breath support, oral focus, and body language all become part of reaching the audience to build performances that evoke emotional responses. And dare we say... standing ovations. Everything you learn about projection will assist you as an actor and in life. Projection takes self-confidence. Self-confidence, in turn, is a big component in becoming a successful performer. Next time you have the opportunity to see a stage performance, study the actors onstage. Watch how the best performers seem to attract the audience from the way they move, how they use their voices to bring the script to life, and how they project their characters to the entire theater.

Projection
Exercise #28

This time, add the proper breath support and breath management that we have learned previously. As you practice this phrase, remember to stay in character, maintain the energy with the enunciation, and use the lyric accents and syllabic stress. With all these elements, you will be able to project and be heard!

Now join the class as they work on vocal projection on Track 28.

GLEE Vocal Method #29 ———
Full Performance – "Sing!"

Okay, it's time to put all these concepts together. Use "Sing!" to go beyond singing. Challenge yourself to turn this exercise into a performance. Choose someone to take the other role and go for it! Be a performer! Be an entertainer!

Cue up Track 29 and get ready for your standing O!

CHAPTER 8
Telephone

Song #8 "Telephone"

This next song takes us from the lofty artistic heights of the Broadway stage to the street life and the club scene as imagined by Stefani Joanne Angelina Germanotta. Who? Oh, that's right... you probably know her as Lady Gaga. Whatever you want to call her, she is one of the most influential artists on today's music scene. She does it all: great pop song writing, technically trained piano skills, strong vocal chops, total immersion into performance art and theatricality. Doing it all has catapulted her to the top of the music world in just a few years.

This song was recorded for Lady G's second release, an EP titled *The Fame Monster*. As you can guess from the album title, this song laments the other side of being famous. For Gaga, that means everyone wanting some of her time and attention, even when she's at the club having fun dancing with her friends.

GLEE's version of "Telephone" is very faithful to Lady Gaga's version. Do you remember the first season's finale? The entire season builds up to New Directions competing at Regionals. Sadly, they suffer a disappointing loss. Season 2 opens with Rachel Berry trying to recruit new singers so that the Glee Club will have a better chance of winning. Often on GLEE, guest stars are brought on to help develop the story line. Enter Charice Pempengco, the young Filipina vocal phenomenon whom Opera Winfrey called "the most talented young singer in the world."

Charice plays foreign exchange student Sunshine Corazon whom Rachel identifies as a possible new member for the club. But it all goes awry when Rachel encounters Sunshine in the girls' bathroom and they sing an impromptu duet of "Telephone." Rachel is intimidated by Sunshine's performance. Rachel, being Rachel, knows there is room for only one diva. She identifies Sunshine as her competition and tries to sabotage her audition.

Study this excerpt of lyrics from "Telephone" and see if you can find the right "street-style" attitude for your solo.

> Hello, hello, baby, you called? I can't hear a thing.
> I have got no service in the club, you see, see.
> What, what, what did you say, huh? You're breaking up on me.
> Sorry, I cannot hear you. I'm kind of busy, kind, kind of busy.

Sorry, I cannot hear you.
I'm kind of busy.
Can call all you want, but there's no one home,
And you're not gonna reach my telephone.
Out in the club and I'm sippin' that bub,
And you're not gonna reach my telephone.

GLEE Vocal Method #30 ──────────
Key Concept: Singing with Attitude

Part of being a GLEE-worthy singer is to be able to change styles and adapt your native vocal style to other idioms with grace and ease. "Telephone" is a wonderful example of what we call "street style." What we mean by that is the collision of multi-cultural trends and musical influences forming new pop music sounds. "Telephone" borrows elements of style from rap and hip-hop music. It also incorporates the street slang of young people who drop the full pronunciation of complete words and mix street jargon phrases that have a different meaning than their traditional usage. Like "bad" meaning good, both "hot" and "cool" meaning the same thing, "destroy" meaning to do something well. Take that, Mr. Webster!

Also, what's hip in this song is the use of the cell phone and texting as devices to showcase the "stutter singing" that has been a style for as long as Rap has been around to become the lyrics and phrasing of a pop, hook-laden, top-selling song.

If you've been studying classical music or vocal jazz, this is your chance to break loose and develop some "street cred" as you work on stutter singing.

Singing with Attitude
Exercise #30

Practice this phrase from "Telephone" with the exaggerated consonants—specifically, the repeated Ks in the word "kind." Emphasize these Ks with attitude and confidence! Remember that attitude is directly related to the groove of the tune and the subdivision of the eighth notes. You can also over-enunciate the Bs in "busy" and the C in "cannot." Repeat this over and each time keep exaggerating the enunciation of these consonants. Have a lot of fun with this!

kind, kind of bus - y,   kind, kind of bus - y.   Sor - ry, I can-not hear you. I'm kind of bus - y.

Are you ready to go clubbing? Not so fast! First please join Kate and the class as they work on street attitude on CD Track 30.

GLEE Vocal Method #31 ———
Key Concept: Group Rap Singing

This lesson may be a challenge to singers who look down on hip-hop artists because they don't really sing. But the reverse is often true as well: Good singers may not be adept at rapping—or, as we call it, rap singing. In our studio work, we've seen ultra-talented vocalists become shy and inhibited as they try to emulate the sound of rappers and hip-hop musicians.

Here's tip #1: Rap singing needs a variety of pitches to sound authentic. Some voice actors call this "roller coaster" style. You go up, then down, the up pitches being for emphasis and down pitches for creating conclusions or periods... kind of like riding a roller coaster. All of these up and down vocal shifts are on indefinite pitches. More importantly, they are in rhythm, much like a drummer taking a solo.

Tip #2: You need projection like we were working on in lesson #28. It's hard to be timid and take this stance. You need the utmost self-confidence to perform in this style. So if you're feeling shy, channel your inner rapster!

Near the end of "Telephone," the entire glee club joins Sunshine in speak-singing the hook. This is a great place for you to practice this style. So put down your cell phone, and no texting while rapping—I mean speak-singing!

Group Rap Singing
Exercise #31

This exercise is designed to get you out of your shell if you have inhibitions about rapping or don't even know where to start! Like the other rap singing exercise, you get to choose the pitches you want, but in this case you should remember the context in which we are performing—more "street" and R&B-inspired vocals. The first time, you can utilize a single pitch value. But remember you are speaking this! As in the previous exercise, you should be aware of the subdivisions in the melody line and the enunciation of the consonants. Overall, let's hear your attitude!

Let's catch up with Kate and her crew as they work on their street "cred." Cue up CD Track 31 and do it with attitude!

GLEE Vocal Method #32 ———
Key Concept: Finding Indefinite Pitches for Rap Singing

For singers who have not done much rapping (And who are we kidding? That's probably most of you.), finding good indefinite pitches to build your performance on is essential. In this lesson, we're going to work on building another key vocal skill that GLEE singing uses: the rap-singing step-out or a rap-style solo.

Choral music has many examples of chanting or singing with indefinite pitches. Think about it: Even Gregorian chants have some of these semi-sung techniques that sound both ancient and timeless. In the 1960s, artists such as Gil Scott-Heron and the Last Poets used rap singing in a mash-up of jazz and R&B that many music historians look to as Ground Zero for the burgeoning art form of rap. Jumping forward to around 1970 in the Bronx area of New York City, a fusion of

African-American and Puerto Rican styles converged in block parties. This style soon became popular in the local clubs, being way more "up from the streets" than disco.

The earliest rappers were actually the MCs (master of ceremonies) and they led these street social events. These early artists had a mastery of the improvisational rhyming that sounds somewhat like a drum solo with lyrics. Lady Gaga's song "Telephone" uses this approach in the last section of the song. It tells a story with quick-sounding lyrics that are sung with indefinite pitches. The high and low points sound much like an exaggerated form of speaking, but in a rhythm that is evocative of the funky drums in dance music.

This lesson will help you grab the center of attention like the MCs of the rap world as you find high and lower pitches sung in rhythm. Now that you have sung with the group in exercise #31, let's use that same section of "Telephone" to practice your solo turn as a rapper.

Indefinite Pitches for Rap Singing
Exercise #32

This time you will get to improvise more and really reveal your inner rapper! The example below is one option you could use. It follows the contour of the original melody line. Treat these as indefinite pitches and make sure the text is heard in an interesting and stylistically effective way! Repeat this two-measure phrase over and over until you get comfortable with the many versions that are possible. You get to "be" someone every time! Again, be aware of the subdivisions in the melody line and the enunciation of the consonants. Try experimenting with dynamics and accents as well. Most important: Have fun!

Are you ready to take your solo? Let's join the class as Kate helps the students find cool pitches for their rapping step out. Cue up Track 32 and be the MC!

GLEE Vocal Method #33 ——————
Full Performance – "Telephone"

It wasn't by accident that "Telephone" is the last song in the book. It incorporates so much of what we've been learning and lets you put into practice all those exercises you've worked so diligently on: singing solos, singing with a group, speak singing, and performing a step out rap style solo. We know you have!

More than anything else, we hope we've inspired you with the *Glee Vocal Method & Songbook* to be the best performer that you can be. There is almost nothing better than making music with your friends. You now have eight songs in a variety of styles that allow you to put on your own performance with others or by yourself.

Use the Glossary of Vocal Learning to help you learn the concepts of vocal study and the language that vocal coaches use. If you've enjoyed the GLEE vocal experience, consider taking a lesson from a teacher in your town. Do it! Nothing can speed up your ability to become a GLEE-worthy performer than taking lessons.

Finally, check out the suggestions in the section on using microphones and P.A. systems. There are many ideas there that can help you put on a more effective show, using the CD tracks included with the book. We want you to have a great time with music. That's what it's all about!

Cue up Track 33 on your CD.

Now it's your turn to put all these skills together. And don't just sing... Become an unofficial cast member on GLEE... Put on a PERFORMANCE!

(Instrumental)

CHAPTER 9
Staging & Choreography

If you're reading this now, you've worked through all the chapters and have participated in all of Dr. Kate Reid's vocal classes. Right?

No?

Well, we know how tempting it is to skip ahead. But if you haven't learned all the singing techniques, choreography moves and microphone techniques won't do you much good. So, go back and finish... We'll be here waiting for you.

Staging Concepts

Now we're ready to start planning a performance. We're going to give some simple, easy-to-execute concepts for the eight songs. But first, let's step back from the microphone and talk about staging and performance concepts. Everything in this book empowers you to start performing by your self—right now! All you need is a boom box or a computer with speakers. Put the CD in the disc player, select a song, and you're ready. But if you want to perform with other singers, well, that's another story... er, performance. But it's easy! Just remember this: Never more than three people on a mic.

Simple, right?

If you just want to sing with your friends and don't ever plan to perform, feel free to sing in any configuration you like. But if you plan to sing in front of real people—aka the audience—you're going to need techniques that use microphones and a P.A. (public address) system as part of your performance. In that case, practicing this staging concept gets you started with easy, logical ways to expand, using geometric patterns that look good to the audience.

Guidelines for Staging

- There must be a designated solo mic (or solo position, if no mics are being used) that is the pre-set place for the soloist to perform, as well as another mic for the group. (See Diagram 1, page 69.)
- Singers in the group, including the soloist before and after soloing, share one mic per three singers. When a solo comes, the soloist moves to the solo mic. If an entire song is a solo, the soloist can start at solo position. If a second singer is singing a duet section of the song, the second singer should move to the solo mic and share the mic with the opening soloist.
- The solo mic is positioned center stage and the second mic is to the right or left and slightly behind the solo position. (See Diagram 1.)
- If there are six singers, three mics are needed for this staging and should be set-up in a triangle formation, with the soloist mic at the top of the triangle facing the audience. If you have as few as three singers, this is still the best staging. (See Diagram 2, page 69.)
- Two non-solo singers can share a mic, but never more than three. So, if we have nine singers, we need at least four mics. Twelve singers need five mics, with the center stage microphone designated for soloists. (See Diagram 3, page 69.)
- Use non-boom, straight mic stands. Each mic must have a mic clip that easily allows it to be pulled off the stand to be handheld. Not only do straight stands look less cluttered, they

allow the singers more room to change positions around the mic and do some of those great choreography moves. (More about those later.)

- When a soloist finishes, move back to one of the group mics so that the solo mic will be open for the next soloist.

Guidelines for Soloing

- Look at the audience—not at your feet, not at the ceiling, not at the walls. Find someone in the audience to sing to. That person becomes a proxy for the entire audience.
- Be completely in the moment. You can worry about washing the dishes or cleaning your room some other time. Now the only thing that matters is putting on a show—and you are the center of attention!
- Use your entire body as an extension of your voice. In other words, don't just stand there: Perform!
- Know the song really, really well. As a GLEE-worthy singer, it's not acceptable to forget your lyrics, sing the wrong melody, or look bored, scared, or unsure. If you have studied the *Glee Vocal Method & Songbook*, you know that finding the soul-stirring underpinnings of the song is at the heart of your presentation. Singing and acting then come together in perfect synergy while the emotional center, the meaning of the song, flows through you to become a performance that would impress Rachel or Finn, or any of the singers in New Directions.

Guidelines for Singing in the Choir

- Move and feel the music. If your choir has a choreographer, use their direction to craft a great stage performance, but don't overshadow the soloists.
- Smile when you sing, unless the dramatic center of a song is serious or sad. If the song has a sadder tone or message, work for intensity in your face without creating tension in the jaw, neck, or throat.
- Blend with the other singers. Do not sing loud just to hear your own voice.
- Focus your eyes on the audience in the same way the soloist does. The exception to this rule is if someone is singing a solo. In that case, focus your visual energy toward the soloist. This will dramatically channel the attention of the audience to specific aspects of the performance.
- Never "pull focus." That is, don't make your performance as a group singer bigger or more dramatic or more eccentric than the rest of the choir.

Choreography

Choreography is an important adjunct to the *Glee Vocal Method & Songbook* in crafting a great performance. Hal Leonard Corporation has many books that can teach you how to move with the best of them. Several of them are written by our friend John Jacobson, one of America's best-known and most respected show choir choreographers. John breaks down movement to music using easy-to-digest key phrases such as "reach for the stars," "walk in time," and "opera hands." Perhaps you've heard his most famous phrase, "double dream hands." Three million YouTube hits later, it has gone on to become a viral smash hit.

Go to the Hal Leonard website (www.halleonard.com) and check these out:
Gotta Sing, Gotta Dance: Basics of Choreography and Staging (HL08745825)
John Jacobson's Riser Choreography (HL08745827)
Decades of Dance DVD (HL09970644)

One of John's choreography concepts is to allow choir members to "free style" during certain segments of a song. Free style means that, interspersed with sections of a song that are uniform and synchronized, choir members can do their own thing in other parts of the song. Not only is this is a great way of kick-starting your performance into the Gleek-mosphere, it will also get you used to moving while singing.

We suggest making one of your fellow performers, especially the best dancer in your group, the dance captain of your group. This is just what happened with GLEE: Actress/dancer Heather Morris, who plays Brittany, was one of the choreographers before joining the cast.

But before you break out your dancin' shoes, here are a few key points to remember when you are moving and singing together:

- Always be aware of your upper body, neck, and head position. Remember that proper vocal technique should not be compromised when choreography is added to the performance. Choreography should always enhance the overall experience for the audience and not detract from the musical elements of the performance. The diaphragm and ribcage need proper posture in order to take in and manage your air for efficient and healthy breath support and tone production. Be careful of choreography that creates tension or tightness in and around the neck and shoulders. We want to maintain a relaxed feeling in these areas of the body at all times.
- Keep your face forward to the audience.
- Diction is often the first thing to go when movement is added. Make certain that you are concentrating on delivering the lyric or story at all times.
- It's easy to forget the vocal lessons we learned! One way to check and see if you're maintaining the lessons is to assess your overall "feeling" after performing: You should not be experiencing vocal fatigue. Proper breath support and management, along with efficient tone production and resonance, will allow you to sing for a reasonable amount of time. It is very important to consider all the vocal elements of the performance along with the choreography!

Finally, tap into that great musical archive that we call YouTube. Performances by almost every great singer or group are only a click away. We recommend that you start your performance by copying the moves of other great performers and singing groups. As you progress, make it your own, do your thing, be original. To get you started, we have some easy staging ideas for each of the songs that will get you moving right now!

Staging Concepts for "Don't Stop Believin'"

For this song, we are going to use three singers around two mics. The mics can be considered stage positions if you perform without mics. This staging uses the triangle setup shown in Diagram 2, page 69.

1. All singers on group mics for opening vocals.

2. Male soloist moves to solo mic for first solo.

3. Female soloist moves to solo mic and takes next solo while male singer moves back and joins choir.

4. All singers on group mics during transition, then male and female soloists move to solo position, taking turns on mic as they sing. They share the solo mic for duet section, with the group vocalists singing backing vocals on their mics.

5. Guitar solo: All singers move free style. Do your own dance moves that fit the song.

6. Male and female soloists on solo mic, all backing singers on their mics until end of song. On the last note, everyone "reach for the sky." (See Diagram 4, page 70.)

Staging Concepts for "Keep Holding On'"

This song falls into the "breaking the rules" category, because four supporting singers are going to share the right mic or right position in the triangle. If your group has more than three mics, this song can be helped with an additional microphone and stand.

1. The four backing singers start the song on the right mic in the triangle as the male and female soloists enter from opposite sides.

2. The soloists take the mic off the stand in the left and solo positions and hold their mics, while the backing singers keep their mic on the stand on the right. Backing singers keep their eyes on the first soloist.

3. Backing singers move their arms from high to low as they sing the high-to-low ah's.

4. Soloists free style their movements and direct their performances to each other and the audience and do not look at the backing singers.

5. After the first chorus, the soloists sing second verse directly to each other, in close proximity.

6. Continue this approach until end of the song.

7. As the two soloists come to the last words, the entire group and soloists focus their gaze at the floor and bow their heads and the song is over. (See Diagram 5a and 5b, page 70.)

Staging Concepts for "To Sir, With Love"

1. Female soloist approaches the solo mic during the instrumental intro.

2. Backing singers come onto their mic positions just before they sing with soloist on the chorus.

3. Female soloist stays on solo mic while male sings duet on second verse on the left mic. He should be exactly in the center of the mic position, with the other backing singers on each side of him.

4. Backing singers rejoin on their mics on second chorus.

5. At the end, when the soloist is finished, all singers stand motionless as the instrumental finishes. (See Diagram 6, page 71.)

Staging Concepts for "Hello, Goodbye"

This song also breaks the rules, but in reverse. Backing singers all share the left mic in the triangle. If you have more than three mics and more than six singers, try having the backing singers go to two singers per mic.

1. As the instrumental intro plays, the male soloist moves to the front of the triangle and takes the mic off the stand to handheld performance style.

2. As the male vocalist sings, the female soloist moves to the right mic in the triangle and takes the mic off the stand in handheld performance style.

3. As the soloists perform, they do not look at each other, but look instead at someone in the audience.

4. After the second chorus, the soloists finally face one another as they sing, "You say yes, I say no..."

5. For the rest of the song, the soloists sing to each other as they bring to life the duality that is the essence of Paul McCartney's classic lyrics.

6. As the soloists sing, the backing singers walk in place in time to the music, with girls focusing their look at the male soloist and the male backing singers focusing their gaze on the female soloist. (See Diagram 7, page 71.)

Staging Concepts for "Can't Fight This Feeling"

1. The male soloist comes to the solo mic during the intro and sings the first verse.

2. All backing singers are on the left and right mics behind the soloist in the triangle. The singers do not face the soloist. Instead, they face each other. As the soloist comes to the first chorus, the backing singers face forward toward the soloist. At the end of the first chorus, the backing singers return to looking at each other in a motionless state, not pulling focus from the solo singer.

3. At the beginning of the next chorus, the backing singers look forward, directly at the male soloist as he sings the rest of the song. At the end, they resume their stoic stance and face each other as the song finishes. (See Diagram 8, page 71.)

Staging Concepts for "Lean on Me"

1. The entire choir comes to the front solo mic and sings the gospel style intro, snapping their fingers on beats 2 and 4.

2. The male soloist and the female soloist each are on the back mics. They sing with the choir from that position in the intro.

3. The male soloist takes the right mic off the stand and assumes handheld performance style, coming up to the front line, with the choir on the far right.

4. Before the start of the first chorus, the female soloist takes the mic off the left stand and assumes handheld performance mode, standing in a straight line with the other singers. The male soloist puts the mic back on the stand.

5. After the first chorus, a female singer from the choir moves to the center solo mic and takes the gospel-style solo. The choir moves to the two other mics while she is centerstage.

6. The female soloist stays in center position while the scat answer singers move to the center of the outside mics on the straight line. They perform their step-out answers from this position, with the choir members standing close around them.

7. In the third chorus, all singers (except the soloist) start gospel hand claps on beats 2 and 4 while they step time in place.

8. On the third verse, the male soloist moves to the center mic, trading places with the female soloist.

9. At the conclusion of the false ending, the female gospel soloist moves to the center mic and finishes out the song in this position. (See Diagram 9, page 72.)

Staging Concepts for "Sing"

1. The triangle formation stays, but the soloist moves the center mic straight back from in front of the left and right mics and positions the solo mic behind, reversing the triangle. The backing singers move their mics to face the soloist, singers on the left, singers on the right. The idea here is to give all the backing singers the role played by Tina, now a choir or Greek Chorus. The soloist plays the role of Mike. This song could also have a female soloist as it is performed in the original Broadway show, *A Chorus Line*.

2. The entire song is performed in this formation, with the soloist acting out their predicament of not being able to sing.

3. When the choir sings "caroling," referring to Christmas caroling, the singers use John Jacobson's "opera hands," bringing both hands to the chest and clasping them together.

4. At the last note, all the singers raise both hands to the sky for the applause moment. (See Diagram 10, page 72.)

Staging Concepts for "Telephone"

1. During the soft intro, the soloist moves to the center mic and the backing singers move to the two mics on the left and right of the triangle formation.

2. The soloist performs from the center mic.

3. Backing singers move to the music in free style hip-hop moves until their support vocals are needed. They immediately stop moving and face the mic and the audience to sing the section of the song, then back to free style after the part is sung. The backing singers appear not to acknowledge the lead vocalist, as if they're at a dance club.

4. When the song gets suddenly soft before the out choruses, the backing singers freeze and become motionless—sometimes called "vogueing"—assuming model-like poses seen in fashion shows.

5. Backing singers do free style as the song resumes the dance beat.

6. In the last section, all the singers do the rap-sing in unison, walking in place to the beat of the song. As the rap-sing repeats, all the singers go to free style hip-hop moves.

7. At the end of the song, all singers freeze in place as the softer music plays to the end. (See Diagram 11, page 73.)

Glee Vocal Method Legend/Symbols

⌄ = directional mic   ✕ = mic stand

∨ = arrow shows which direction the mic picks up sound

⊗ = singer   ⟋↗↖ = movement

Diagram 1

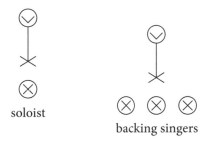

AUDIENCE

soloist

backing singers

Diagram 2

AUDIENCE

solo mic

Diagram 3

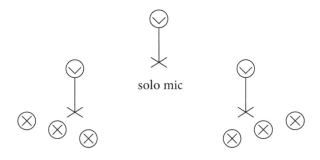

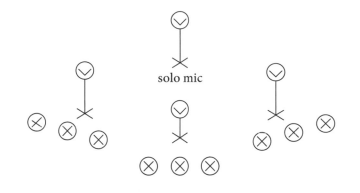

AUDIENCE

solo mic

Diagram 4 – "Don't Stop Believin'" Staging

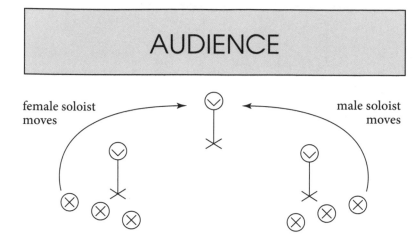

female soloist
moves

male soloist
moves

Diagram 5a – "Keep Holding On" Staging

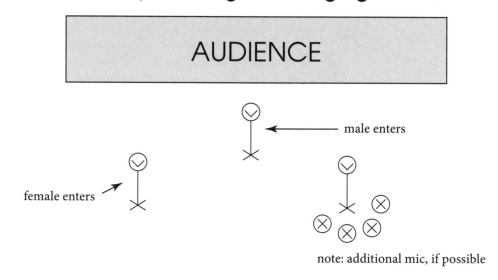

male enters

female enters

note: additional mic, if possible

Diagram 5b – "Keep Holding On" Staging

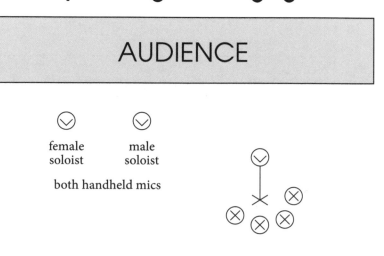

female
soloist

male
soloist

both handheld mics

Diagram 6 – "To Sir, With Love" Staging

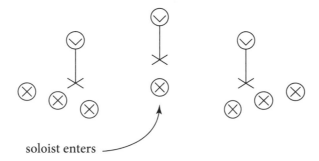

soloist enters

Diagram 7 – "Hello, Goodbye" Staging

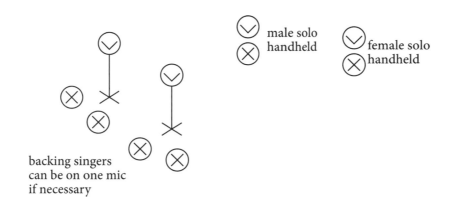

male solo
handheld

female solo
handheld

backing singers
can be on one mic
if necessary

Diagram 8 – "Can't Fight This Feeling" Staging

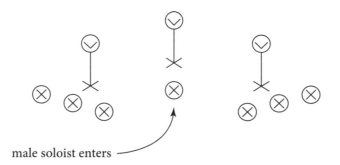

male soloist enters

Diagram 9 – "Lean on Me" Staging

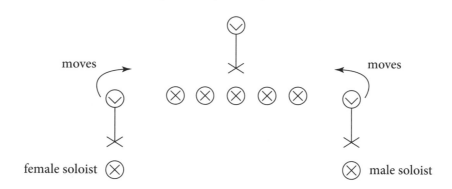

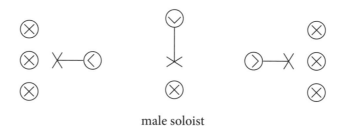

Diagram 10 – "Sing" Staging

Diagram 11 – "Telephone" Staging

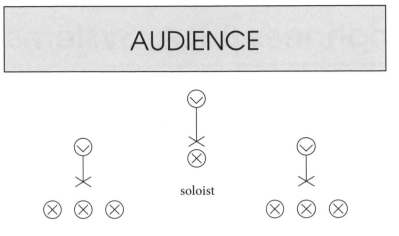

Diagram 12 – Large Ensembles Up to 30 Singers

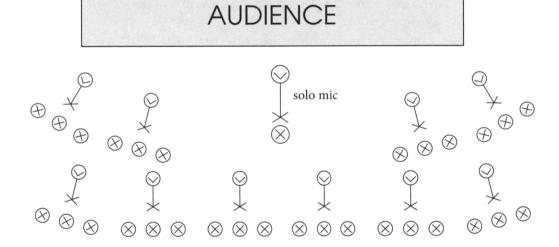

CHAPTER 10
Using Microphones & P.A. Systems

One of the best concepts of the *Glee Vocal Method & Songbook* is that you can sing along to tracks that sound exactly like those you've heard on GLEE. All you have to do is insert the enclosed CD into your closest CD-playing device. Yes, that's you singing, sounding just like a Gleek. But as you progress into performance situations with a live audience, you'll need to learn additional skills about the use of microphones and P.A. systems.

Most performers call this skill set "mic technique." This chapter will discuss some of those techniques.

Let's step back from the mic for a second and look at the long history of musical performance. Using microphones and amplification is a fairly new development as far as singing goes. Until the 1920s, all singing was completely acoustic. Cabaret, Broadway, vaudeville, opera, and more intimate, musical styles of "parlor singing" relied on the vocal projection of the singer. As the swing era and the dance bands of the 1930s became popular, these bands started featuring vocalists as an addition to the instrumental sounds of this dance driven jazz music. Early jazz singers used megaphones to project their voice over the wind and rhythm instruments.

But as amplification was invented and improved during the 1920s and '30s (using some of the same technology invented for radio), singers started to use microphones to be heard above the big band. Ultimately, this led to singers developing a completely new kind of singing. This resulting style sounded more intimate to the listener. Singers could now convey the lyric and the meaning of the songs without needing to sing at the top of their lungs to be heard above the band.

Bing Crosby completely reinvented his sing-to-the-back-row style by using a softer approach that harnessed the power of amplification. This allowed him to sing in a soft, intimate tone that put him right at the front edge of the sound of the band. Soon, younger singers of the era such as Frank Sinatra based their entire vocal styling on this up-close-and-personal model. Today, every singer that stands in front of a mic—including you—shares this legacy from the swing era of the 1930s and '40s.

Another facet of the microphone's influence in popular music is the reality that all recordings and all broadcast mediums such as radio, TV, and movies are completely dependent on microphones to pick up the sound. Through time, listeners have come to expect this close-mic'd, amplified sound as the standard for how singers are heard in any performance.

Look at the cover of this book. What do you see? A singer holding a mic. So read on and we'll share a few mic secrets of the pros. Like them, you will gain an understanding of how all this technology fits into your overall performance.

Basic Microphone Guidelines

1. Always use a cardioid mic for your vocals. Cardioid means that the mic picks up sound in a pattern shaped like a heart and that the mic rejects sound from the rear and the sides. Look at the mic on the cover of this book and visualize a balloon coming from the front of the mic where you sing. That imaginary balloon resembles the pickup pattern of a typical

cardioid (directional pickup) mic. This is really important because the sound that comes from the speakers can create feedback, that annoying squealing sound that you sometimes hear with amateur performances. Directional mics suppress feedback and help make vocals sound clearer and more defined. There are many different brands of mics; today, most brands have similar products. The microphone on the cover of this book is a Shure SM-58. It is the industry standard for live vocal mics. If you need a mic for your next gig, the SM-58 is a great one to start your performing career with.

2. Work the mic close, but not too close. In our Glossary of Vocal Terms, one of the items to learn and know is "Proximity effect." This refers to the fact that directional mics add bass response as you work the mic closer. Working the mic close gives you added frequency content in your lower range and makes your voice sound richer and fuller. But beware: It also can make you sound muddy and unintelligible to the audience. Learning exactly where to put the mic in front of your mouth takes practice.

3. Use a mic stand. Many performers feel they always have to hold the mic in their hand to deliver a great performance. We recommend that you practice using a mic on a stand and then take the mic off when it adds intensity to your performance. Review the staging concepts in appendix 2 to get ideas about this concept.

4. Don't block your face with the mic. Remember that the audience wants to see your face and your facial expression as you sing. The mic will pick up your voice really well if you place the mic directly in front of your chin, pointing up at your mouth. The same rule applies, whether the mic is handheld or on a stand. This approach also helps control loud plosive consonants like the rumbling Bs and Ps that are distracting to the audience.

5. Back away from the mic if you are going to sing really loud. Your voice will sound better through a P.A. if you move back from the mic when you are belting. But if you are singing softly, get close to the mic. This closeness will give you the intimacy that makes softer vocal production connect with the audience. Professional performers know they can control their mic volume by moving their handheld mic away from their mouth when they belt. The intensity is still there, but the audience hears a more pleasing vocal.

6. Once your performance setup has more than five mics, someone in the group needs to be named "sound guy/girl," aka Ms. Technology or Mr. Sound Mixer.

   Every musical group has at least one member who is interested in sound technology. That person should take leadership in shaping the mix of the microphones. We believe that every musical group should always include a "sound check" prior to a live performance. The designated "sound mixer" is the one to lead this. The sound mixer designate must make sure the audience is hearing what the group wants to present. This group member also may be the best person to communicate with a house sound person at a performance venue.

   Also, remember that, as you perform to pre-recorded backing tracks, the volume level of the tracks is extremely important. If the tracks are too soft, the sense of rhythms and musical texture start to be lost. But, if the tracks are too loud, then all the subtleties of your vocal performance may be lost. Your sound check is the best time to get this right—before the audience shows up!

7. If your group uses more than five mics, you may want to recruit a dedicated sound person who doesn't sing onstage. Today, entertainment technology is becoming an important area of study for musically inclined students who don't desire to be a stage performer. Running the disc player, balancing the mics, fighting feedback problems, even running the lights

has become an important role for a non-performing ensemble member. Many performing groups have found that the b right person mixing the group can be instrumental in helping a GLEE Club or a pop vocal group become artistically and financially successful.

If you want to learn more about live sound and entertainment technology, Hal Leonard has many wonderful books and DVDs that will magnify your knowledge. One resource that is perfect for the young or aspiring sound mixer is Bill Gibson's *The Ultimate Live Sound Operator's Handbook*, a 384-page tome with an accompanying instructional DVD (HL00331469).

APPENDIX
Glossary of Vocal Terms

Balanced onset: Occurs when the vocal folds are brought together in conjunction with the application of the breath. This type of attack does not engage the throat muscles, but instead utilizes the diaphragmatic management of air, along with the proper use of the vocal fold musculature.

British invasion sound: A tone that generally uses a lower resonance like the mouth and with little vibrato, if any. For diphthongs, this style generally stays on the initial vowel sound and releases with the suggestion of the second.

Broadway sound: A tone that is achieved through a forward, "in the mask" resonance and clear enunciation. Depending on the musical content or character, a quicker vibrato may also be used.

Controlled belt: The belting area in the women's voice is generally just over the break (*passaggio*). It is sometimes called the "chest voice." Using proper resonance, placement, and breath support allows one to sing in this register with a controlled sound.

Controlled vibrato: Using consistent air and proper breath support, this type of vibrato is stable and maintains intonation, style, and timbre (tone color).

Consistent air: Air that maintains its strength and flow while singing on a vowel sound.

Country sound: A tone that is commonly referred as a "twang." This tone can range from nasal resonance to that of the pop sound. The pronunciation of the lyric in this style often goes directly to a continuant consonant or the second vowel sound in a diphthong.

Delayed vibrato: Most often used on long, held notes, this vibrato is added just before the release of the tone.

Diaphragmatic breathing: Using the diaphragm muscle in order to produce consistent air and maintain breath support. Sometimes referred to as "breathing low," diaphragmatic breathing is optimal. On the other hand, clavicular breathing—not using the diaphragm but rather expanding only the lungs—will not provide the proper support necessary.

Diffused tone: A vocal sound that is not quite focused, but not entirely breathy. It is used with laterals vowels, consistent air, with or without vibrato.

Diphthong: Two adjacent vowel sounds occurring within the same syllable. Technically, a diphthong is a vowel with two different targets; that is, the tongue moves during the pronunciation of the vowel.

Enunciate: To say a word clearly.

Exaggerated vowels: Vowels that are shaped beyond what is considered normal speech.

Forward focus: The placement of the resonance of the vocal tone in the mask of the face. How high or low the focus depends on the register of the vocal line. Generally, this focus relates to resonance in or near the nasal cavity.

Glottal attack (hard attack): Heard when the vocalist initiates a tone by first bringing the vocal folds together and then applying the breath. The result is an explosive tone. Also called a "glottal stop."

Gospel sound: A tone that is generally achieved by the use of mouth resonance, delayed vibrato, and "sing it as you say it" diction.

Gospel vibrato: Generally produced on lateral vowels with a flatter tongue over long, held notes. The vibrato tends to be quicker than other vocal styles like jazz, but not as fast as the vibrato used in classical vocal styles.

Handheld mic volume: Refers to the level of sound needed for a handheld mic. The volume required for a handheld mic is less than that for stage mics or floor mics.

Hushed intensity: Technique whereby the vocal line is sung at a quieter volume but maintains intensity and energy with extreme diction, articulation, and dynamics.

Hyper diction: Careful and specific enunciation of the text as it relates to the rhythm of the vocal line.

Lateral vowels: Vowels that are sung as they are spoken in the English language. Generally, the tongue is flatter and the mouth is more closed.

Microphone blend: How voice parts are arranged around a mic for the optimum blend.

Pop sound: A tone that can utilize a wide variety of resonances and amount of diffusion. Depending on the era, the pop sound can have a great deal of gospel vibrato or none at all.

Pronunciation: The way in which a word is pronounced.

Proximity effect: Refers to the distance between the vocalists and the microphones. The type of microphone, the distance from the mic, and number of vocalists sharing a microphone will affect the sound that is achieved from it.

Rap style: A "speak-singing" style, along with the element of a more casual, informal, or vernacular way of speaking. Indefinite pitches are used, and the prosody of the language, the syllabic stress, and emotion of the lyric are all intertwined.

Syllabic stress: The emphasis of various syllables within a given word.

Tall vowels: Creating an open and free vocal sound on vowels such as ah, oh, and eh by dropping the jaw and maintaining a lifted soft palate.

Sing it as you say it: The reasonable and appropriate stress of the syllables in multi-syllabic words. Literally, the text is sung as the words would be spoken.

Speak-singing: A vocal performance on unassigned pitches that has speech-like inflections, logical syllabic stress, and that does not sound trained.

Syllabic stress: The emphasis of certain syllables in a word.

Singing on the consonant: Usually refers to singing through continuant consonants like "m," "n," and "ng." Specific popular music styles utilize this concept.

Singing on the vowel: Most often refers to long, held notes on words that end with a consonant. Maintain the tone on the vowel and place the final consonant just before releasing the tone.

Soft attack: Occurs when too much air pressure is used, so that the vocal folds do not meet to close the space between them. The result is a breathy tone.

Straight tone: A vocal tone without vibrato, maintained by proper breath support and tone placement.

Vibrato: The regular pulsating change of pitch. It is used to add expression to vocal and instrumental music. Vibrato is typically characterized by two factors: the amount of pitch variation ("extent of vibrato") and the speed with which the pitch is varied ("rate of vibrato").

Vocal projection: The ability to create a vocal sound (sung or spoken) that can be heard from a distance.

ABOUT THE AUTHORS

DR. KATE REID is the head of the Pop & Jazz program and chair of the Music Department at Cypress College in Cypress, California. She leads the pop/jazz vocal ensembles, teaches history and styles classes, and maintains an active private voice studio. Kate holds a Bachelor of Music degree in Jazz Studies from Western Michigan University (1992) and Master of Music (1996) and Doctor of Musical Arts (2002) degrees in Studio Music and Jazz Performance (Vocal) from the University of Miami. She is in demand as a clinician and adjudicator for various show choir, choral and jazz festivals throughout the U.S. and Canada.

Kate has extensive experience working with Royal Caribbean and Costa Cruise Lines, recording their Broadway and musical theater style shows. She has also worked as a singer/dancer for Walt Disney World and Cedar Fair Parks and has sung with many noted pop and jazz artists.

Kate's experience as a studio vocalist in Hollywood includes work on films, commercial spots, and backing vocals for various artists. As a jazz singer and pianist, she appears regularly with her quartet at jazz venues all over the Los Angeles area. Her *Sentimental Mood* CD has received extensive airplay on terrestrial radio throughout the U.S. and has been heard on Sirius/XM as well. Her subsequent release, *The Love I'm In* (summer 2011), features more selections from the Great American Songbook.

ANDY WATERMAN is a music producer and recording engineer/mixer working in Los Angeles. His career has put him in the studio with some of the best singers of all time, including Julie Andrews, David Byrne, Brian Wilson, Mel Tormé, Jack Jones, Andy Williams, Bernadette Peters, Cheryl Crowe, and Fergie.

In addition, Andy's studio sessions often feature some of the most accomplished studio singers in L.A., Chicago, Nashville, and New York, including several who perform as backing and interstitial music vocalists on the Fox TV Show GLEE. Throughout his career he has been the music director for large-scale, live stage productions. These shows are featured in theme parks such as Universal Studios and at corporate events for clients including Apple Computer, Intel, Boeing, and Home Depot. He has directed and recorded the vocals for thousands of national TV commercials and radio station IDs heard all over the world.

Recently, he has collaborated in the studio recordings of Tony Award-winning Broadway composer Jason Robert Brown.

Andy is the Creative Director and CEO of Umbrella Media Inc.